W9-BDD-962

Look What You Can Make With

Recycled Paper

◇◇

Edited by Betsy Ochester

Photographs by Hank Schneider

Highlights for Children, Inc.
Honesdale, Pennsylvania

Craft Coordinator
Kathy Ross

Craft Makers
Kerry O'Neil
Kathy Ross

Contributors

Debra Boyles	Helen Kitchell Evans	Lory MacRae
Doris D. Breiholz	Clara Flammang	Carol McCall
Joyce T. Buckner	Kelly McCumber Freihofer	R.C. McIntyre
Tera Burgundy	Norah Grubmeyer	Beth Mehall
Betty Burt	Nan Hathaway	Ouida Johnston Moore
Frances M. Callahan	Deborah L. Hogshead	Kathy Ross
Blanche Campbell	Jerry Holcomb	Sally E. Stuart
Catherine Carmody	Carmen Horn	Sherry Timberman
Marie E. Cecchini	Olive Howie	Marion Ullmark
Patricia Coon	Tama Kain	Carol E. Vogel
Mary Curtis	Lillian Koslover	Francis Wales
B. J. Deike	Elizabeth Searle Lamb	Mary Zook
Donna Dowdy	Lee Lindeman	

Highlights for Children
PO Box 18201
Columbus, Ohio 43218-0201
Printed in China through Colorcraft Limited, Hong Kong

Library of Congress Control Number: 2012955105
Originally published in 2001 as *Look What You Can Make With Newspapers, Magazines, and Greeting Cards*

Books in this series originally designed by Lorianne Siomades
The text of this book is set in Avant Garde Demi. Titles are set in Gill Sans Extra Bold.

10 9 8 7 6 5 4 3 2 1

Getting Started

This book is filled with fun, easy-to-make crafts, and each one begins with old newspapers, magazines, or greeting cards. You'll find a wide variety of things to make, including toys, games, and gifts.

Directions

Before you start each craft, read the directions and look closely at the photograph, but remember—it's up to you to make the craft your own. If we decorate a craft with markers but you want to use glitter paint and stickers, go for it. Feel free to stray from our directions and invent new crafts.

Work Area

It's a good idea to keep your work area covered. Old newspapers, brown paper (from grocery bags), or old sheets work well. If you're creating papier-mâché, you might want to use an extra-thick covering of newspaper for your work area. (Papier-mâché is messy.) Also, protect your clothes by wearing a smock. A big old shirt does the job and gives you room to move. Finally, remember to clean up when you've finished.

Materials

You'll need a lot of old magazines, greeting cards, envelopes, calendars, and newspapers, so start saving now. Ask friends and relatives to help. Keep your craft-making supplies together, and before making each craft, check the "You Will Need" list to make sure you have everything. In this list we will often specify a certain kind of printed paper. For some crafts, however, more than one kind of paper will work. Look at the type of paper used for the craft pictured, and see what you might have on hand that is similar. Also, since you'll need scissors, glue, tape, or a stapler for almost every craft, we don't list these supplies.

Other Stuff

When we show several similar crafts, we'll often list numbered directions that apply to all of the crafts, then specific directions for each craft. When you start a craft made from printed paper, make sure that the magazines, catalogs, greeting cards, calendars, and newspapers you will use are no longer wanted by the original owner.

That's about all. So choose a craft that you like, check your paper stash to find what you need, and have some fun. Before you know it, you'll be showing everyone what you made with newspapers, magazines, and greeting cards.

Papier-mâché Banks

Save your coins in one of these characters.

You Will Need:

- newspaper
- measuring cup
- water
- flour
- mixing bowl
- round balloon
- plastic-foam egg carton
- masking tape
- paint and paintbrush
- pompons, yarn, buttons, and other trims
- old compact disc (CD)
- felt
- chenille stick
- large and small paper cups
- paper plate
- sponge
- plastic wiggle eyes
- cardboard ring
- paper

This project is extra-messy, so use lots of newspaper to cover your work area.

To Make the Basic Bank

1 Tear lots of newspaper into strips.

2 Mix 1 cup of water with 1 cup of flour to make a paste.

3 Blow up the balloon to the size you want your bank to be and knot it.

4 Dip the newspaper strips in the paste, and lay them on the balloon. Cover the balloon with three to four layers of strips. Leave the knot of the balloon uncovered. Let the project dry completely on the egg carton.

5 When the paper ball is dry, pop the balloon and remove it. Cover the hole with masking tape to close it.

To Make the Mouse Bank

Paint the ball in your favorite mouse color. Glue a pompon over the area where the balloon was removed to make the nose. Cut a coin slot in the top of the mouse. Glue the mouse to the CD to keep it from rolling to the side. Cut round eyes and ears from felt, and glue them to the head. Wrap the chenille stick around your finger to make a spiral tail. Glue it to the back of the mouse. Secure the tail with masking tape over the glue. Paint the masking tape. Decorate the body with felt.

To Make the Fish Bank

Tape the small paper cup over the covered hole to form the nose. Cut fins and a tail from a paper plate. Tape them in place. Cut a 1-inch ring from the rim of a large paper cup. Glue and tape the bottom of the fish to the ring to make a stand. Cut a coin slot in the top. Paint the fish. When it's dry, add a light speckled layer of paint in another color by dabbing it over the fish with a sponge. Use the sequins to give the fins and tail some sparkle. We glued buttons under the plastic wiggle eyes.

To Make the Clown Bank

Paint the papier-mâché ball, and let it dry. Cover the cardboard ring with felt or paper to make a collar. Cut a coin slot in the back of the head. Glue the ball to the collar with the covered hole down in the ring. Add a bow tie or other decorations, if you wish. Glue on yarn hair. Glue a cup hat on top of the hair. Decorate the hat. Use trims to give the clown a face. This clown has a felt smile, a pompon nose, and eyes made from felt, buttons, and sticker stars.

More Ideas

Other characters are easy to make. Try a bear, or a porcupine with chenille-stick quills. Make different-shaped fish to turn your room into a tropical sea.

Newspaper Dolls

Make a fashionable friend or two to play with.

You Will Need:

- newspaper
- paper towel
- masking tape
- paint and paintbrush
- yarn
- plastic wiggle eyes
- beads, buttons, and other trims
- fabric scraps
- ribbon
- chenille stick
- paper baking cup
- artificial flowers

1 Crumple half of a single sheet of newspaper into a ball for the head. Cover the ball with a paper towel, and hold it in place with masking tape.

2 To make the body, fold a single sheet of newspaper in half from top to bottom. Then roll the sheet from the fold to the end. Secure the newspaper roll with glue. Do the same thing with another sheet.

3 Glue the two rolls together in an X with the top of the X slightly shorter than the bottom. Secure the two rolls in the center with masking tape while the glue dries. Attach the head by taping the excess paper towel to the center of the X. Bend the arms down, and glue them at the fold.

4 Paint the doll, and let it dry.

5 Use the yarn to make hair. Paint on shoes and a face, or use plastic wiggle eyes and other trims. Cut a rectangle of fabric to form both the front and the back of the dress. Cut a slit in the center. Slip the head through the slit. Tie the dress at the waist with ribbon.

To Make the Basket

Glue the ends of a chenille stick to each side of a paper baking cup. Glue artificial flowers in the basket. Glue the basket to the doll's arm.

More Ideas

Cut the toe from an old sock to make a hat. Roll the cut edge to make a brim, and glue a pompon on the top.

String some beads for the doll to make a necklace and a bracelet.

Switch-Plate Decoration

Make every light switch bright.

You Will Need:
- greeting card
- switch plate
- pencil
- masking tape

1 Glue the front and back of the greeting card together.

2 Remove the switch plate from the wall, and trace around it on the card. Don't forget to trace around the rectangle for the switch.

3 Cut out the new cover from the card.

4 Attach the cover to the switch plate with a small roll of masking tape.

More Ideas

Save special cards to make covers for each season.

Flowery Card

Send this card to someone you love.

You Will Need:
- thin cardboard
- magazines or catalogs

1 Cut out the letters that spell "Mom" or another name from the cardboard.

2 Cut out pictures of flowers from magazines or catalogs.

3 Glue the pictures on the letters. Trim around the edges.

4 Glue the letters to a folded piece of cardboard. Write a message inside.

More Ideas

Make a card for your sister or aunt using pictures of flowers she likes best.

Neat Note Holders

Display your messages in style.

You Will Need:

- greeting cards and magazines
- thin cardboard
- spring-type clothespins
- thin ribbon

To Make the Note Holder

Select a picture from a greeting card or a magazine, and carefully cut it out. If necessary, glue the picture to thin cardboard to make it stiff. Glue the picture to one side of a spring-type clothespin with the bottom of the picture at the handle end of the clothespin. Stick a note in the clothespin.

To Make the Line of Birds Note Holder

Glue a picture of a bird to a clothespin with the feet of the bird touching the tip of the pinching end of the clothespin. Slip flower pictures from cards or magazines behind each bird, and glue them in place. Tie a length of ribbon from wall to wall, and clamp the birds across the ribbon.

More Ideas

Glue a magnetic strip on the back of the clothespin, and stick a note holder to the refrigerator.

Make note holders for dinner guests, and put a place card in the holder at the table.

Call Grandma

Hang birthday or other greeting
cards from your Line of Birds
Note Holder.

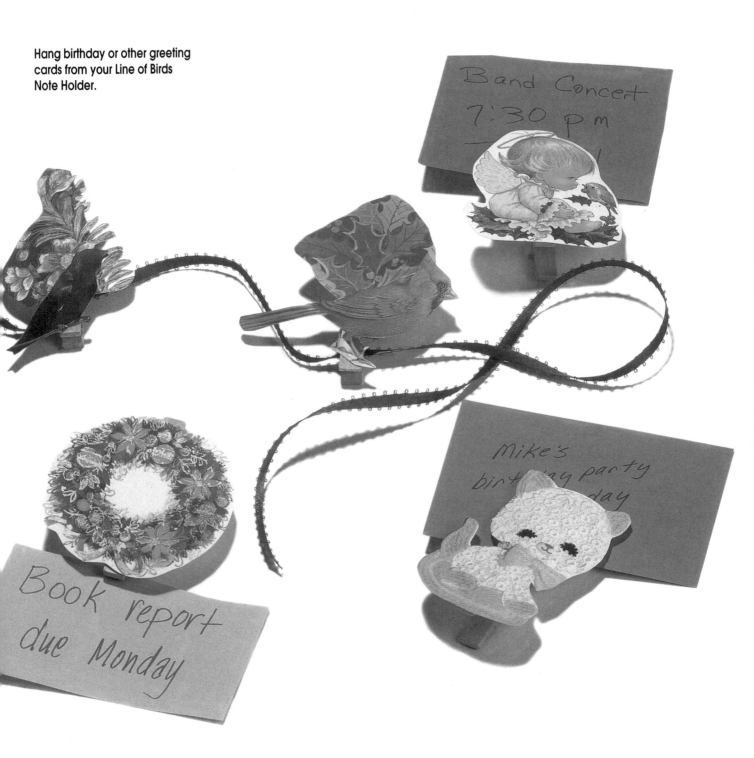

Papier-mâché Mouse

This little critter has a body made of newspaper.

You Will Need:

- newspaper
- measuring cup
- water
- flour
- mixing bowl
- plastic-foam egg carton
- paint and paintbrush
- beads, pompons, thread, ribbon

This project is extra-messy, so use lots of newspaper to cover your work area.

1 Tear the newspaper into strips.

2 Mix 1 cup of water with 1 cup of flour to make a paste.

3 Wad a piece of newspaper to make a mouse base. Twist one end of the base to make the tail.

4 Dip the strips of newspaper into the paste, and wrap them around the base, shaping the mouse as you wrap. Cover the base with several layers of strips. Add folded strips at the head for ears. Cover the ears with more layers of pasted newspaper. Let the mouse dry on the egg carton overnight or until completely hard.

5 Paint the mouse. Add a face using trims. This mouse has tiny bead eyes, a tiny pompon nose, thread whiskers, and a ribbon bow on the tail. How will you decorate yours?

More Ideas

You can use this technique to make other animals. How about a sleeping dog or cat, or maybe a bird?

For some extra painting fun, add something decorative to the animal, such as a small painted flower on the side.

Covered Gift Box

Make this little gift box for someone special.

You Will Need:

- toothpick box
- magazine or calendar picture
- pencil

2 Place the flattened box upside down on an interesting or colorful part of the picture. Trace around the box, and cut the shape out.

3 Glue the cut picture to the outside of the box.

4 Reassemble the box and reglue the edges.

More Ideas

Add a sticky-back Velcro closure to the box so you can use it to store tiny toys.

1 Carefully take the toothpick box apart at the places where it is glued. Flatten the box out.

Car Carrier

Stash all your small vehicles in one place.

You Will Need:

- half-gallon milk carton
- magazines
- hole punch
- yarn or chenille stick
- colored plastic tape

More Ideas

Make a carrier for any kind of small item. Once you decide what your carrier will hold, look for pictures of those objects to cut and paste.

1 Cut the top off the milk carton and discard it.

2 Cut out lots of pictures of vehicles from old magazines.

3 Glue the pictures all over the outside of the milk carton.

4 Punch a hole on the opposite sides of the carrier. Attach yarn or a chenille stick through each hole to make a handle.

5 You can cover the top edge of the carrier with colored plastic tape to give it a more finished look.

Greeting Card Mobiles

Display your holiday cards in a special way.

You Will Need:

- ribbon
- greeting cards
- yarn
- wire coat hanger
- hole punch
- craft beads
- jingle bells

To Make the Greeting Card Mobile

Cut different lengths of ribbon. Cut one large picture from a card, cutting through the back panel. Glue the card together with the two ends of one ribbon in between to form a hanger and the other ribbons hanging down from the bottom. Cut around the pictures, including the back panel, of other greeting cards. Glue the front and back of each card together with a ribbon in between. Hang the cards at different heights so they do not cover each other. Trim off any excess ribbon sticking out from the bottoms.

To Make the Valentine Mobile

Tie pieces of yarn across the hanger. Punch a hole in the center of the top and bottom of each card. String the valentines onto the yarn. String beads in between some of the cards. Tie off the end of each piece of yarn with a bead or a jingle bell. Arrange the cards along the yarn so they are evenly spaced. Use tape on the back of any cards that slip on the yarn. Slide some beads over the hook. Secure the top bead with glue. Cut two cards the same size. Glue the two cards, back to back, over the hook. Tie a bow at the top.

More Ideas

Instead of a wire hanger, make a base from two craft sticks. Glue the sticks in the center to form an X, then hang ribbon or yarn from the ends.

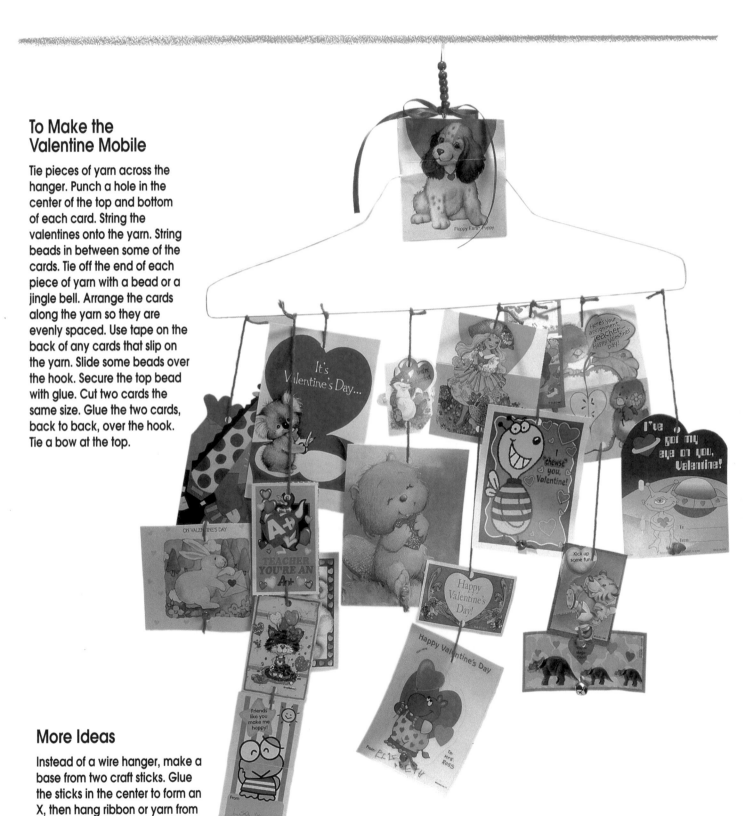

Newspaper Nelson

This friend is big enough to have his own chair.

You Will Need:

- newspaper
- yarn
- construction paper
- trims

4 Staple the top closed. Add yarn for hair as you staple. Create a face and other details using construction paper and decorative trims.

More Ideas

Use markers or paint to create the face and clothes. How can you make your Nelson unique?

1 Open six double sheets of newspaper, and stack them together. Three of the sheets will form the front of Nelson, and three will form the back. Staple the sheets together around three sides. Leave the top open for stuffing and room for the arms and legs.

2 Roll a single sheet of newspaper for each arm and leg, securing the roll with staples. Insert the legs and arms into the body.

3 Stuff Nelson with balls of crumpled newspaper between the front three sheets and the back three sheets.

Stamp-Covered Paperweight

Start saving those stamps to make this beautiful paperweight.

You Will Need:

- canceled stamps
- water
- waxed paper
- rock
- paintbrush
- felt

1 Cut the stamps from envelopes. Soak them in water to remove them from the paper. Put the wet stamps on the waxed paper to dry.

2 Glue the stamps to the rock. Paint the stamps with glue to seal and protect the edges.

3 Cut a piece of felt to cover the bottom of the rock. Glue the felt in place. This will keep the paperweight from scratching your desk.

More Ideas

Glue magazine pictures to the rock instead of stamps. Seal with glue.

Ribbon Picture Holder

Display art from three favorite greeting cards.

You Will Need:

- white poster board
- three greeting cards
- clear glitter
- ribbon
- notebook ring

1 Cut three circles from white poster board.

2 Cut a picture from a greeting card to glue on each circle. Cover each circle with glue, press the picture in the center, and sprinkle the rest of the gluey circle with clear glitter.

3 Cut a long strip of ribbon. Cut a triangle shape from the bottom end to make two points.

4 Staple the top end of the ribbon into a loop. Put a notebook ring through the loop.

5 Glue the three pictures to the ribbon.

More Ideas

Make seasonal holders for spring, Thanksgiving, or Hanukkah.

Papier-mâché Hat

Your tops in this wacky hat.

You Will Need:

- large paper bag
- pencil
- poster board
- masking tape
- measuring cup
- water
- flour
- mixing bowl
- newspaper
- paint and paintbrush
- ribbon and other trims

This project is extra-messy, so use lots of newspaper to cover your work area.

1 Put the bag on your head. Roll up the opening of the bag until it's the height you want. Cut the rolled-up portion from the bag.

2 Trace around the opening of the bag on the poster board. Draw a larger circle around this one to make a brim, and cut it out. Tape the brim to the bag hat.

3 Mix 1 cup of water with 1 cup of flour to make a paste. Tear lots of newspaper strips. Dip the strips in the paste, and lay them on the hat. Cover the hat with two to three layers of strips. Let it dry completely.

4 Paint the hat, then decorate it with trims. As the hat dries, pull it out a little on the sides. Or find a bowl that is about the size of your head. Turn it upside down and cover it with plastic wrap. Slip the hat over the bowl. This hat dries very hard, so you want to be sure the bag dries in a shape that will fit over the top of your head.

More Ideas

Instead of painting the hat, use a layer of colorful magazine pictures or construction paper cut in strips for your final surface.

Greeting-Card Place Cards

Any dinner table is special when you add a set of these place cards.

You Will Need:

- ruler
- thin cardboard
- construction paper
- greeting cards
- markers

1 For each place card, cut a 3-inch square from the cardboard. Fold the square in half.

2 Cover the folded place card with construction paper.

3 Cut a small picture from a greeting card. Glue the picture to the card.

4 Use the markers to write the names of your guests.

More Ideas

Create place cards for different holidays, such as Thanksgiving, Christmas, or Passover.

Jellybean Basket

This little basket makes a great party favor.

You Will Need:

- greeting cards
- pencil
- plastic margarine-tub lid
- hole punch
- thin ribbon

1 Cut a picture from a greeting card. Trace around the lid on the card to make a circle. Cut the circle out.

2 Cut four 1½-inch slits, equal distance apart, in from the edge of the circle to make four flaps. Punch a small hole in the top edge on each side of one flap. Do the same thing to the flap directly across from the one you first punched.

3 Thread one end of a ribbon through the hole on one side of the first flap. Thread the other end of the ribbon through the hole on the opposite flap. Tie the ribbon in a bow, pulling the circle up to form one side of the basket. Do the same thing on the other side.

4 Cut a strip from another card for a handle. Glue it inside the basket. Glue decorations on the handle.

More Ideas

Fill the basket with paper grass and add goodies.

Start with a larger lid to make a larger basket.

Old Glory Collage

Make this flag to hang on your door for Independence Day.

You Will Need:

- white construction paper
- magazines
- cardboard
- twine

More Ideas

Use sticker stars instead of cutting out stars.

Make a smaller version of the flag on construction paper. Hang this outside during your Fourth of July picnic.

1 Cut a square of white construction paper to mark off the blue section on the flag. (Do not glue it to the cardboard.)

2 Glue red pictures from the magazines over the cardboard. Stop at the upper left-hand corner where the blue section will be.

3 Cover another sheet of white paper with white pictures. Cut the paper into six white strips. Glue them to the flag. If the strips are too short, cut more strips to add to them.

4 Cover the white square with blue pictures cut from the magazines. Trim the edges. Glue the blue square to the upper left-hand corner.

5 Cut thirteen stars from yellow pictures. Glue the stars in a circle on the blue square. Glue the ends of a piece of twine on the back.

Super Storage Holders

Organize your magazines, mail, and other stuff.

You Will Need:

- sturdy box with lid
- brown paper
- magazines and calendars
- pasta box
- large cardboard box
- colored plastic tape
- pencil
- construction paper
- hole punch

To Make the Storage Box

Cover a box and lid with brown paper. Once you decide what the box is to be used for, cut out pictures from magazines and calendars that remind you of the contents. Glue just a few pictures over the box, or cover the entire box with a collage of pictures. Can you guess what is stored in the box shown?

To Make the Basic Holder

1 Cut the sides of the box partway down at a slant, then cut across the front of the box to remove the top.

2 Cut pictures from magazines and calendars. Glue them to the box.

3 Give the edges a finished look by covering them with the colored plastic tape.

To Make the Mail Holder

Cut letters that spell "mail" from a magazine. Glue the letters across the front of the box. Trace around the back of the box on construction paper. Cut paper to fit in the back of the inside of the box, and glue in place. Do the same thing on the bottom of the box. Punch a hole in the back for hanging.

To Make
the Magazine Holder

Make sure your box is large enough to hold your magazines. Glue on pictures from old issues or other pictures that you like.

More Ideas

Make a picture-covered container on pages 28 and 29 to match your magazine and mail holders for a neat desk set.

Notebook House

Design a house of your very own, then use cutout figures to tell a story.

You Will Need:

- magazines and catalogs
- large notebook
- markers
- fabric, wallpaper, wrapping paper
- paper clips
- greeting cards
- masking tape

1 Cut the furniture and details for each room from old magazines and catalogs.

2 You can make the top part of each notebook page the wall and the bottom part the floor. You can cover the wall and floor by coloring with markers or gluing on pieces of fabric, wallpaper, or wrapping paper.

3 Arrange the cutouts in a way that you like, then glue them in place in the notebook.

4 Stand the notebook up. Open to the room you wish to use. If the pages do not stay open, secure them with paper clips.

To Make the Stand-Up Figures

Cut small pictures of animals and people from the greeting cards. Bend the outer loop of the paper clip down to make the clip stand. Use the masking tape to attach a figure to the front of the paper clip that sticks up. The bent part of the paper clip should be behind the figure.

More Ideas

You might want to make the storage box on page 20 to keep the notebook house and cutouts until you are ready to use them. Store your stand-up figures in there, too.

New rooms can be added to the notebook house over time.

Card Gift Tags

Select some favorite figures from your greeting card collection to make gift tags.

You Will Need:

- greeting cards
- hole punch
- embroidery thread

1 Cut a picture from the greeting card.

2 Punch a hole in the top.

3 Cut a length of thread, and knot the two ends together. Thread the loop through the hole in the picture, then thread the opposite end of the loop through itself to secure the tie to the tag.

More Ideas

A set of these tags in a plastic sandwich bag tied at the top with a pretty ribbon makes a welcome gift.

Moving-Picture Cube

Here is an unusual way to display your pictures.

You Will Need:

- construction paper
- magazines or greeting cards
- two reinforcement rings
- yarn

1 Cut six identical squares from construction paper. Fold the corners to the center, making a smaller square. Unfold the corners. Glue a favorite magazine picture or greeting card in the center of each square.

2 Glue the four squares together, side by side. Glue a square to the bottom.

3 Poke two holes in the center of the last square, about an inch apart. Put a reinforcement ring over the back of each hole. Thread a piece of yarn through the two holes, and tie the ends together for a hanger.

4 Glue the last square to the top.

More Ideas

This is a good way to display photographs, too.

23

Deck the Halls

Save your holiday cards to make one-of-a-kind decorations.

You Will Need:

- thin cardboard
- aluminum foil
- magazines
- ruler
- pencil and pen
- holiday greeting cards
- ribbon and other trims
- paper
- plastic wrap
- hole punch
- paper clips
- jingle bells

To Make the Twelve-Day Christmas Calendar

Cover the cardboard with aluminum foil. Tape the foil in the back. From magazines, cut out the number twelve and the letters that spell "days of Christmas." Glue them across the top of the calendar. Make a 2-inch square pattern from cardboard. Use the pattern to trace and cut twelve colorful picture squares from the greeting cards. Glue the bottom and side edges of each square to the calendar. The top should be open, like a pocket. Tape a piece of ribbon to the back of the calendar. Cut twelve 1-by-4-inch strips of paper. On each strip write your "gift" for the day, one gift for each of the twelve days of Christmas. Gifts can be words of love and support, ideas for family holiday fun, or promises to do extra chores. Fold each paper strip "gift" in half, and tuck it in one of the pockets of the calendar.

To Make the Christmas Card Wreath

Cut a 2-by-4-inch rectangle from the back of one card. Trace around the pattern on eighteen to twenty cards. Cut the traced rectangles out. Arrange the rectangles in a circle, overlapping each other, on a piece of plastic wrap. Glue the cards in place. When the glue has dried, peel the wreath from the plastic wrap. Glue a loop of ribbon to the back. Add a bow to the front.

To Make the Paper-Clip Garland

Cut small pictures from the cards. Punch a hole on both sides of each cutout. String the pictures together with paper clips slipped through the holes. When the garland is as long as you want it, slip a jingle bell on the paper clip at both ends.

More Ideas

You might want to add other decorations to your calendar, such as sequins, glitter, or curls of ribbon.

You can make the wreath for spring using flowery cards.

Try cutting smaller rectangles to make a tiny wreath to hang on a Christmas tree.

Invite your friends to help make the garland. See how long you can make it.

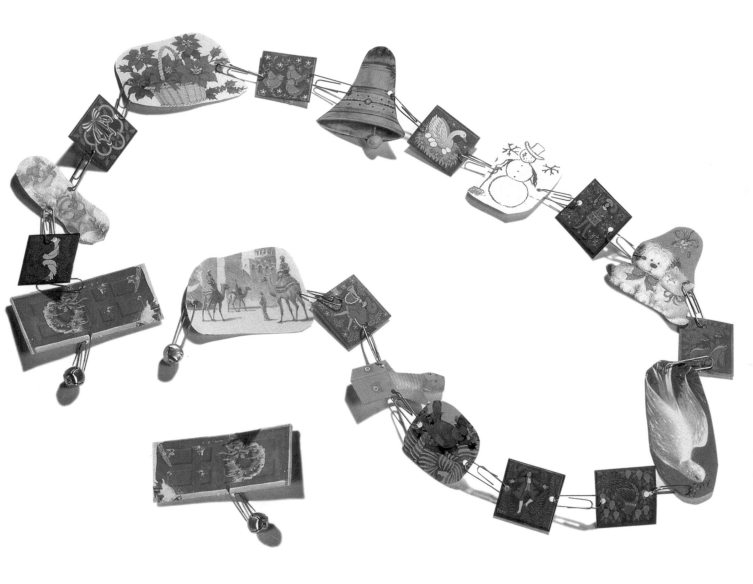

Picture Pins and Rings

Design your own jewelry.

You Will Need:

- greeting card
- jewelry pin
- clear nail polish
- chenille stick

Choose a picture from a greeting card to use for the pin or ring. Cut the picture out.

To Make the Pin

Attach the jewelry pin to the back of the picture. Cover the front with clear nail polish to protect it.

To Make the Ring

Wrap one end of the chenille stick around your finger, twisting the ends together to make a ring that fits. Trim off the extra chenille stick. Glue the picture on the ring where the two ends of the chenille stick are joined.

More Ideas

If you do not have a jewelry pin, try a small safety pin. Glue the back of the pin to the back of the picture, using masking tape to hold the pin in place while the glue dries.

Add tiny details to the pin or ring by gluing on sequins, craft jewels, and other trims.

Newspaper Ned

Roll some old newsprint into a puppet.

You Will Need:

- newspaper
- markers
- construction paper
- pompons and other trims

1 Close a double sheet of newspaper, and roll it into a puppet. Tape or staple the roll to secure it.

2 To make hair, cut slits in the paper and fluff them out.

3 Add a face and details using markers, paper, and other trims.

More Ideas

Make arms from newspaper, and staple to the sides.

Felt Travel Box

This felt board makes a long trip more fun.

You Will Need:

- felt
- shoe box
- magazines and catalogs

1 Cut a piece of felt to fit inside the lid of the shoe box, then glue it to the lid.

2 Cut pictures of people, animals, and objects from the magazines and catalogs.

3 Glue each picture to felt. Let the glue dry. Trim around the edges of each picture.

4 Use the pictures to make scenes on the felt-lined lid. When you are not playing with the pieces, store them in the box.

More Ideas

Decorate the outside of the box with cutout pictures from magazines or greeting cards. Cover with glue to seal.

Custom Containers

Cover simple containers in different ways to hold your toys and other treasures.

You Will Need:

- magazines and catalogs
- plastic or cardboard containers
- ribbon and other trims
- pencil
- hair pins

To Make the Picture-Covered Containers

Cut out your favorite words or pictures. Glue the pictures over the container. Cover the pictures with a coating of glue to hold down the edges and protect the pictures. Decorate the top and bottom of the container with ribbon or other trims.

To Make the Rolled-Paper Holder

Tear several colorful pages from the magazines. Lay the pencil on one edge of a page.

Squeeze a thin line of glue across the opposite edge. Roll the page around the pencil toward the glued edge. Press the glued edge down to secure the roll. Slip the pencil out of the roll. If the glue is not holding the roll in place, slip a hair pin over each end of the roll until the glue dries. Cut the tubes to the same height as the container. Cover the container with glue, and stick the paper rolls on the container. Decorate with trim.

More Ideas

If the container has a lid, you might want to glue a decorated wooden bead to the center of the lid for a handle.

If you're making a container for a relative or a friend, choose pictures or words that the person would like.

You can use paper rolls to cover any straight-sided container. You can also use them to decorate flat surfaces, such as picture frames or box tops.

Story-Figure Magnets

Write a story, then use your refrigerator as a stage.

You Will Need:
- greeting cards
- magnetic strips

1 Cut figures from old greeting cards.

2 Glue a magnetic strip on the back of each figure.

3 Stick the figures on the refrigerator to use for play and storytelling.

More Ideas

You can also play with your story figures by sticking them on an old cookie sheet.

You might want to add some houses and scenery to your storytelling collection.

Keep your magnets in the storage box on page 20.

Homemade Alphabet

Collect lots of letters to play word games.

You Will Need:

- magazines and catalogs
- thin cardboard
- plastic margarine tub with lid

1 Cut words from the magazines and catalogs. You might want to cut out some punctuation marks, too, such as question marks and exclamation points.

2 Glue the words to thin cardboard.

3 Cut the letters apart.

4 Use the margarine tub to store your letters.

More Ideas

Add more letters to make more words.

Decorate your storage container with pictures or letters.

Magazine Valentine

Try this different idea for making Valentine's Day cards.

You Will Need:

- pencil
- thin cardboard
- construction paper
- magazines
- white paper
- ribbon and other trims

1 Sketch a small heart on the thin cardboard. Cut the heart out to use as a pattern.

2 Make a folded card from construction paper that is slightly larger than the heart pattern.

3 Use the pattern to trace a heart on the front of the card. Cut the traced heart out.

4 From a magazine, cut an area of red or pink color that is slightly larger than the heart. Glue the magazine picture inside the card so that the color shows through the cutout heart. Cut a liner from the white paper. Glue the liner inside the card.

5 Add some ribbon or trim to the front.

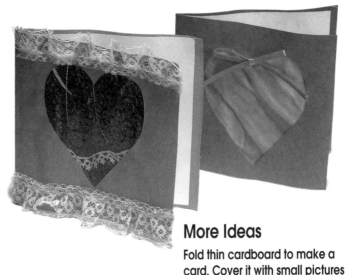

More Ideas

Fold thin cardboard to make a card. Cover it with small pictures in one color or in different colors. Then trace and cut out your heart pattern.

Thanksgiving Centerpieces

Make these impressive turkeys for your Thanksgiving table.

You Will Need:

- round balloon
- measuring cup
- water
- flour
- mixing bowl
- newspaper
- brown paint and paintbrush
- thin cardboard
- poster board
- magazines
- masking tape

This project is extra-messy, so use lots of newspaper to cover your work area.

1 Blow up the balloon and knot the end.

2 Mix 1 cup of water with 1 cup of flour to make a paste. Tear newspaper into strips. Dip the strips into the paste, and wrap them around the balloon. Let dry completely, then pop the balloon and discard.

3 Paint the body brown. When dry, tape a ring of cardboard to the bottom.

4 Cover the poster board with magazine pictures in fall colors. Then cut out a head, two feet, two wings, and lots of tail feathers. Glue the head to one end of the body. Cut eyes and a beak from poster board scraps. Glue them to the head. Cut a wattle from a red magazine page, and glue it so it hangs down from the beak.

5 Glue the two feet to the body below the head. Glue a wing on each side of the body. Secure heavy pieces with masking tape until the glue dries. Spread the tail feathers out in a fan shape, and staple them together at the bottom. Glue the tail feathers to the back of the turkey.

More Ideas

Using the body shape, try making
a swan or a duck.

Designer Envelopes

Turn colorful pictures into eye-catching envelopes.

You Will Need:

- envelope
- calendars, magazines, or catalogs
- pencil
- white paper

1 Carefully unglue the seams of the envelope, and flatten it out to use as a pattern. Place the pattern on a picture so that the picture will be on the front of the envelope.

2 Trace around the envelope, and cut it out.

3 Fold the new envelope exactly as the pattern envelope was folded. Secure the seams with glue. Glue on rectangles of white paper for the address and return address spaces.

4 Use a sticker or glue to seal the flap.

More Ideas

Collect envelope patterns in several sizes, and store them in a zipper-close bag.

Paper Bracelet

Wear this jewelry anytime.

You Will Need:

- newspaper
- acrylic paint and paintbrush
- nail polish

1 Cut sixty-four small hearts from newspaper. Glue four together, one on top of the other, spreading glue over the entire heart. Repeat until you have sixteen sets.

2 With white glue, fasten the top of one heart over the tip of the next, curving them slightly as you work. Coat the bracelet with the glue and let dry overnight.

3 Cover with acrylic paint. When this is dry, decorate the hearts with red nail polish.

More Ideas

Create other shapes for your bracelet, such as seashells or stars.

Marble Maze

Test your skill with this maze game.

You Will Need:

- shallow box or lid
- magazine
- pencil
- plastic drinking straws
- marble or wooden bead
- marker

1 Cover the shallow box or lid with magazine pictures.

2 Tear several pages from the magazine. Roll each page around the pencil a few times. Slip the pencil out and continue rolling the page. Secure the edge of the rolled paper with glue.

3 Design your maze in the bottom of the box using pieces of straws. Make sure the paths are wide enough to allow the marble to pass through. When you are happy with the design, replace the straws with the paper rolls. Use the straws to measure the length of each roll. Glue the rolls to the bottom of the box.

4 Poke a hole in the side to drop the marble through at the beginning of the maze. Write the word "start" near the hole. At the end of the maze, poke a small hole through the bottom of the box so the marble can rest. Write the word "finish" near the hole.

More Ideas

Time yourself to see how quickly you can move the marble through the maze.

Don't forget to make some paths in the maze that lead nowhere.

Puzzling Projects

Homemade jigsaws are fun to put together.

To Make the Jigsaw Puzzle

Cut the poster board to the same size as the picture you are using. Glue the magazine or calendar picture to the poster board.

Let dry. Fold a strip of colored plastic tape over all four sides of the puzzle. Use the marker to draw the shape of each puzzle piece on the back. Divide the puzzle into about twelve pieces. Cut the puzzle apart following the lines. Store the pieces in a zipper-close bag.

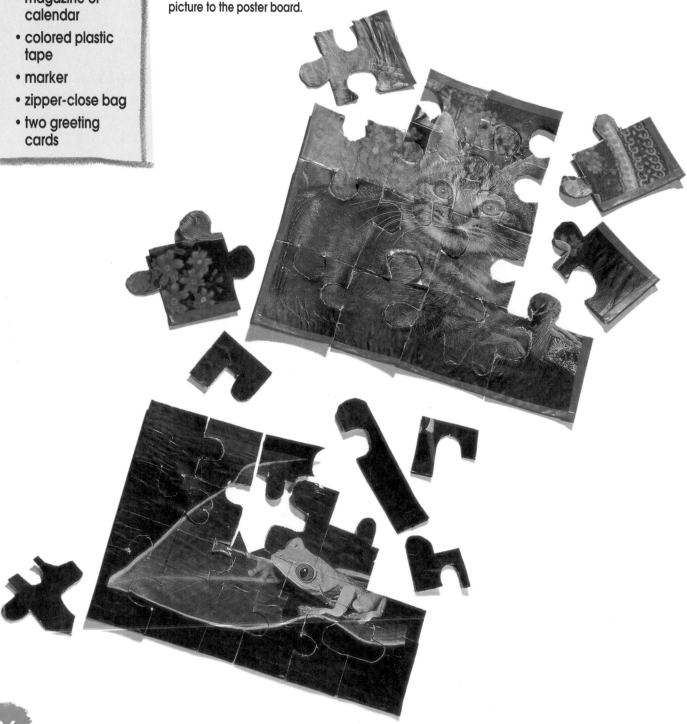

To Make the
Two-Sided Puzzle

Cut the picture off the front of each greeting card. Trim the two pictures so that they are the same size. Glue the two pictures back to back so there is a picture on each side. Let the glue dry before continuing. Cut the pictures into five or six pieces to make a puzzle.

More Ideas

Glue a picture from a calendar or a magazine to a piece of thin cardboard. Cut the picture into horizontal strips. Mix up the strips. Try to put the picture back together.

Happy-Sad Flower Puppet

Turn this flower's face to suit your mood.

You Will Need:

- magazine
- pencil
- thin cardboard
- construction paper
- markers
- hole punch
- metal paper fastener

1 To make the stem, select a magazine picture with lots of green in it. Starting at one corner, roll the page around the pencil four times. Slip the pencil out, and continue rolling to the opposite corner. Glue the corner down to secure the roll.

2 Cut two identical circles from the thin cardboard. Cover them with construction paper. Cut flower petals from yellow-colored pictures. Place one circle color-side down. Glue the ends of the flower petals around the circle. Glue the second circle over the first circle, color-side up.

3 Draw a face on the flower. (Notice how the smile and frown are drawn.)

4 Punch a small hole in the center of the flower and in the top of the stem. Attach the flower to the stem using the paper fastener.

5 Cut leaves from construction paper. Glue the leaves to the stem.

More Ideas

Make four or five flowers in different heights, and put them in a vase.

Doorknob Decoration

Make your door a festive entryway.

You Will Need:
- greeting card
- 12-inch chenille stick

1 Find a greeting card with a large figure or picture that you like.

2 Close the card, and cut the figure out through both the front and back.

3 Glue the front and back of the card together with the two ends of the chenille stick between them so that the chenille stick forms a hanger.

More Ideas

Cut a piece of poster board 4 inches wide and 8 inches long. Measure down from the top of the short side about an inch and draw a 2-inch-wide circle. Cut a slit down from the top to the circle, and cut the circle out. The poster board should now slip over your doorknob. Cut pictures from old magazines to decorate the hanger.

Patchwork Stocking

Fill a paper stocking with your Christmas wishes.

You Will Need:
- construction paper
- magazines and catalogs
- yarn, ribbon, and other trims
- jingle bell
- thin cardboard

1 Cut a stocking shape from construction paper. Cut colorful squares from pictures in the magazines and catalogs.

2 Glue the squares on the stocking to make it look like patchwork. Trim around the stocking. Glue the stocking to construction paper, leaving the top of the stocking unglued.

3 Cut pictures of gifts you are wishing for from the catalogs. Tuck the pictures at the top of the stocking, and glue in place.

4 Glue trim and a loop hanger to the stocking. Glue a jingle bell to the toe.

5 Glue strips of ribbon or trim around the picture. Fold the top of the picture over a strip of cardboard. Tie a long piece of yarn together. Slip part of the loop under the fold to form a hanger. Glue the fold and yarn in place.

More Ideas

Make a two-sided stocking. Add a loop and hang it just like a real stocking.

Works of Art

"Draw" with paper to make your very own masterpiece.

You Will Need:

- greeting cards
- paint and paintbrush
- paper plates or construction paper
- markers
- ribbon, yarn, and other trims
- newspaper comics
- unused crossword puzzles
- cardboard

To Make the Greeting Card Picture

Cut pictures from the greeting cards, and arrange them in a picture. Glue the shapes to a painted paper plate or construction paper. Add details to the picture using markers and trims. Frame your creation by gluing it to a slightly larger plate or piece of paper. Add a ribbon hanger.

To Make the Comics Art

Cut circles, triangles, and other shapes from the comics section of the newspaper. Arrange the shapes on construction paper to make a picture. Glue the shapes to the paper. Use yarn and markers to add details.

To Make the Crossword Mosaic

Create a design in the crossword puzzle by coloring all the blank spaces in different colors. Glue the finished project to cardboard. Cut a piece of construction paper slightly bigger than the puzzle. Glue the puzzle to the center of the paper to create a frame. Glue a yarn or ribbon hanger to the back.

More Ideas

If you look closely at the daily newspaper, you will find lots of things to color. How about the comics section?

Cover both sides of the cardboard-mounted crossword puzzle with clear packing tape, and use it under a vase or as a place mat.

Rebus Letter

Create a picture-and-word message.

You Will Need:
- magazines
- paper

1 Cut out small pictures from the magazines that can represent either part of the word or the entire word. Do this for the whole message you want to create.

2 Cut out letters to finish the words.

3 Glue the pictures and letters to a sheet of paper to write your message.

Can you read our letter?

More Ideas

Create a rebus for your birthday party invitation.

Picture-Perfect Postcard

Here's an idea for reusing old greeting cards.

You Will Need:
- greeting cards made of thin cardboard
- pen or marker

1 Cut the picture panel from the front of the greeting card.

2 On the back of the panel, draw a line down the center to create a message section and an address section.

More Ideas

To create a note card from a greeting card, open the card so that all four sections of the folded card are showing. Cut the card in half, removing the section with the verse and the section next to it. This will leave the card blank for you to write on.

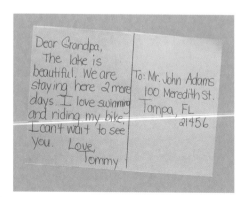

Papier-mâché Puppet Pal

Act out a story with this silly hand puppet.

You Will Need:

- round balloon
- cardboard tube
- masking tape
- measuring cup
- water
- flour
- mixing bowl
- newspaper
- paint and paintbrush
- yarn, buttons, and other trims
- felt

This project is extra-messy, so use lots of newspaper to cover your work area.

1 Blow up the balloon to the size of a tennis ball, and knot the end. Cut a 1½-inch ring from the cardboard tube for the neck. Tape the balloon to the cardboard ring with the knot of the balloon inside the ring.

2 Mix 1 cup of water with 1 cup of flour to make a paste. Tear lots of newspaper into strips. Cover the head and neck form with layers of strips dipped in the paste. Fold pasted strips to stick out on each side of the head for ears. Cover the folded strips with more layers of pasted paper to strengthen them. Add a nose for the puppet in the same way.

3 Let the head dry completely before painting it. Use trims for hair, eyes, and a mouth.

4 Cut a front and back body from felt. Make sure the body is large enough to put your hand in after the seams have been glued. Cut hands for the puppet from felt. Glue the front and back together, with the hands in between. (Do not glue the neck or the bottom together. These need to be left open.)

5 Glue the body to the neck. (You might want to use a rubber band to hold the body in place while the glue is drying.) Decorate the body with cut felt and other trims.

More Ideas

Make two or three puppets, and put on a puppet play with your friends.

Bookmark Bonanza

Make some of these for yourself, or give as gifts.

You Will Need:

- greeting cards
- ruler
- pinking shears
- ribbon
- old envelopes
- canceled stamps
- pencil
- drinking glass

To Make the Zigzag Bookmark

Choose a sturdy greeting card, and cut a rectangle about 2 inches wide and 3½ inches long. Give the rectangle a fancy edge with the pinking shears. Cut two crosswise slits near the top of the card and two near the bottom. The slits should be just wide enough to slip a piece of ribbon through. Cut a 6-inch piece of ribbon. Thread it through the slits at the top and bottom. Cut a triangle-shaped piece out of the ends of the ribbon.

To Make the Corner Bookmark

Cut the corner from the bottom of the envelope. The edge can be straight, or you can create a fancy one. Cover the corner with postage stamps cut from old envelopes or a picture cut from a greeting card. Slip the bookmark over the corner of the page where you stopped reading.

To Make the Medallion Bookmark

Trace around a small drinking glass on two cards. Cut the two circles out. Cut a 15-inch piece of ribbon. Fold the ribbon in half, and glue the circles together back to back, with the fold of the ribbon in between them.

More Ideas

Try making other bookmark shapes, such as a triangle or a square.

Use embroidery thread instead of ribbon.

Newspaper Pumpkins

These jack-o'-lanterns will be around for many Halloweens to come.

You Will Need:

- newspaper
- string
- measuring cup
- water
- flour
- mixing bowl
- orange paint and paintbrush
- twig
- brown chenille stick
- green and black felt

This project is extra-messy, so use lots of newspaper to cover your work area.

1 Crumple two sheets of newspaper into a ball. Tie the ball with string to help keep the round shape.

2 Mix ½ cup of water with ½ cup of flour to make a paste. Tear some newspaper into strips. Dip the strips into the paste, and wrap them around the ball. Wrap the ball with three layers of pasted strips. Let dry, then paint the pumpkin.

3 Poke a small hole in the top of the pumpkin, and glue in a twig for a stem. Wrap the chenille stick around your finger to make a vine. Stick the end of the chenille-stick vine in glue, then into the hole.

4 Cut a leaf from the green felt, and glue it to the stem. Cut facial features from the black felt, and glue them in place.

More Ideas

Two or three of these pumpkins in slightly different sizes make a wonderful Halloween display.

Greeting Card Frame

Here is an easy way to frame your small works of art.

You Will Need:

- greeting card with border
- paper
- colored pencils or markers
- thin ribbon or yarn

1 Cut the picture out of the border of the card.

2 Cut a sheet of paper to fit inside the card. Draw a picture on the paper.

3 Glue the ends of a piece of ribbon to the inside of the card to make a hanger.

4 Glue the picture to the inside of the card, over the ends of the ribbon.

5 Close the card, and glue the frame over the picture.

More Ideas

Write a greeting on the back of the frame, and give your artwork as a gift.

Shaped Notepad

You can make these simple little pads in a hurry.

You Will Need:

- greeting card
- pencil
- white paper

1 Close the card, then cut out the back and front of the card you want to use for the cover.

2 Trace the shape of the cover on the white paper. Cut the paper in stacks of six to eight sheets at a time.

3 Assemble the stack with the front cover on top and the back cover on the bottom. Staple the pad together at one edge.

More Ideas

Add your name on the cover with glue and glitter.

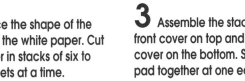
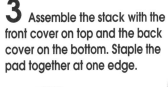

Title Index

Bookmark Bonanza 44
Car Carrier 11
Card Gift Tags 23
Covered Gift Box 10
Custom Containers 28
Deck the Halls 24
Designer Envelopes 34
Doorknob Decoration 39
Felt Travel Box 27
Flowery Card 7
Greeting Card Frame 47

Greeting Card Mobiles 12
Greeting-Card Place Cards . . 18
Happy-Sad Flower Puppet . . . 38
Homemade Alphabet 31
Jellybean Basket 18
Magazine Valentine 31
Marble Maze 35
Moving-Picture Cube 23
Neat Note Holders 8
Newspaper Dolls 6
Newspaper Ned 26

Newspaper Nelson 14
Newspaper Pumpkins 46
Notebook House 22
Old Glory Collage 19
Paper Bracelet 34
Papier-mâché Banks 4
Papier-mâché Hat 16
Papier-mâché Mouse 10
Papier-mâché Puppet Pal . . . 43
Patchwork Stocking 39
Picture-Perfect Postcard 42

Picture Pins and Rings 26
Puzzling Projects 36
Rebus Letter 42
Ribbon Picture Holder 15
Shaped Notepad 47
Stamp-Covered Paperweight 15
Story-Figure Magnets 30
Super Storage Holders 20
Switch-Plate Decoration 7
Thanksgiving Centerpieces . . 32
Works of Art 40

Subject Index

ANIMALS
line of birds note holder 8
papier-mâché-fish bank 4
Papier-mâché Mouse 10
papier-mâché-mouse bank . . 4
Thanksgiving Centerpieces 32, 33

CENTERPIECES
Thanksgiving Centerpieces 32, 33

GAMES
Homemade Alphabet 31
Marble Maze 35
Rebus Letter 42

GIFTS
Bookmark Bonanza 44, 45
Card Gift Tags 23
comics art 40
corner bookmark 44
Covered Gift Box 10
crossword mosaic 41
Designer Envelopes 34
Flowery Card 7
Greeting Card Frame 47
greeting card picture 40
Jellybean Basket 18
Magazine Valentine 31
medallion bookmark 45
picture-covered containers . . 28
Picture-Perfect Postcard . . . 42
Ribbon Picture Holder 15
rolled-paper holder 29
Shaped Notepad 47
Stamp-Covered Paperweight . 15
Works of Art 40, 41
zigzag bookmark 44

HOLIDAY AND OTHER
  DECORATIONS
Card Gift Tags 23
Christmas card wreath 24
comics art 40
crossword mosaic 41
Deck the Halls 24, 25
Doorknob Decoration 39
Greeting Card Frame 47
Greeting Card Mobiles . . . 12, 13
greeting card picture 40
Greeting Card Place Cards . . 18
Happy-Sad Flower Puppet . . . 38
Jellybean Basket 18
line of birds note holder 8
Magazine Valentine 31
Moving-Picture Cube 23
Neat Note Holders 8, 9
Newspaper Pumpkins 46
note holder 8
Old Glory Collage 19
paper-clip garland 25
Patchwork Stocking 39
Ribbon Picture Holder 15
Stamp-Covered Paperweight 15
Switch-Plate Decoration 7
Thanksgiving Centerpieces 32, 33
twelve-day
  Christmas calendar 24
valentine mobile 13
Works of Art 40, 41

STORAGE AND CONTAINERS
Car Carrier 11
Covered Gift Box 10
Custom Containers 28, 29
Felt Travel Box 27
Jellybean Basket 18

magazine holder 21
mail holder 20
Papier-mâché Banks 4, 5
papier-mâché-clown bank . . . 5
papier-mâché-fish bank 4
papier-mâché-mouse bank . . 4
picture-covered containers . . 28
rolled-paper holder 29
storage box 20
Super Storage Holders . . . 20, 21

THINGS TO WEAR
Paper Bracelet 34
Papier-mâché Hat 16, 17
Picture Pins and Rings 26
pin 26
ring 26

TOYS
Felt Travel Box 27
Happy-Sad Flower Puppet . . . 38
jigsaw puzzle 36
Newspaper Dolls 6
newspaper dolls' basket 6
Newspaper Ned 26
Newspaper Nelson 14
Notebook House 22
Papier-mâché Mouse 10
Papier-mâché Puppet Pal . . . 43
Puzzling Projects 36, 37
stand-up figures 22
Story-Figure Magnets 30
two-sided puzzle 37